I0819407

The LIFE *and* MARTYRDOM *of*

SAINT PETER
and
SAINT PAUL

The LIFE *and* MARTYRDOM *of* SAINT PETER *and* SAINT PAUL

Written by

ST. ABDIAS *of* BABYLON

Translated by

Fr. Robert Nixon, OSB

TAN Books
Gastonia, North Carolina

Cover design by Jordan Avery
Cover image: Saints Peter and Paul, Iconostasis in the Greek Catholic Cathedral of the Holy Trinity in Krizevci, Croatia. Image by Zatletic / Adobe Stock.

Interior image on page 2: St. Peter from Christ and the Apostles (woodcut print). Harris Brisbane Dick Fund, 1924 / Metropolitan Museum of Art, CC0, via Wikimedia Commons. Public domain.
Interior image on page 74: St. Peter from Christ and the Apostles (woodcut print). Harris Brisbane Dick Fund, 1924 / Hans Baldung Grien, CC0, via Wikimedia Commons. Public domain.

ISBN: 978-15051-3702-6
ePUB ISBN: 978-1-5051-4036-1

Published in the United States by
TAN Books
PO Box 269
Gastonia, NC 28053
www.TANBooks.com

Printed in the United States of America

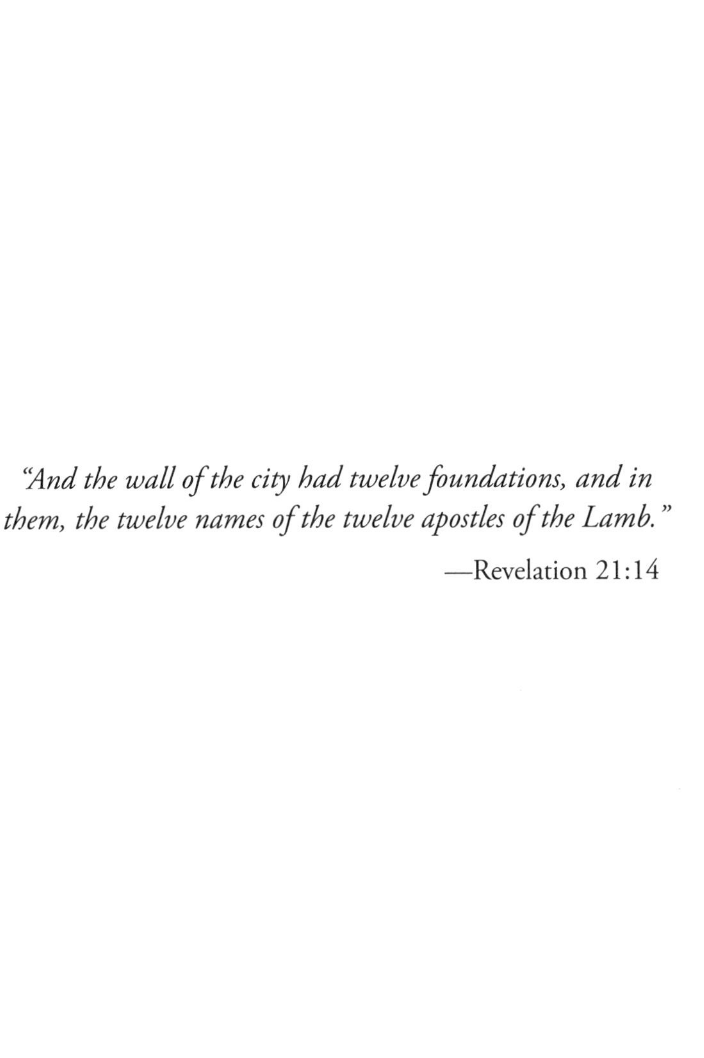

"And the wall of the city had twelve foundations, and in them, the twelve names of the twelve apostles of the Lamb."

—Revelation 21:14

CONTENTS

TRANSLATOR'S NOTE

THE CHURCH VERY rightly honors Saint Peter and Saint Paul as foremost among the apostles of Our Lord Jesus Christ. These two great men were both instrumental in the spreading of the Gospel of salvation, and it was largely thanks to their efforts that the newly founded Church became firmly established in the Mediterranean world, which was the hub of the Roman Empire and consequently the center of the civilized world at the time. Both of these saints preached the Gospel with passionate fervor and unwavering fidelity, and both gave up their own lifeblood as martyrs, in supreme testimony of their own faith and as an eternal witness to the truth of the message which they proclaimed.

Yet surprisingly few contemporary Catholics are familiar with the details of the missionary work and martyrdoms of Saint Peter and Saint Paul in anything but a passing sense. It is true that their martyrdoms are not recounted in the pages of Sacred Scripture—yet this does not mean that we have no reliable knowledge concerning them, any more than the fact that Scripture does not mention Julius Caesar implies that we have no reliable information about him. On the contrary, there are reliable ancient sources that tell us the details of the virtuous undertakings and heroic deaths of these two noble saints. Their lives and work had a major, lasting, and visible effect in the spread of Christianity within the Roman Empire, and consequently the whole course of Western history; their writings are preserved within the New Testament; and the places where they were executed and buried have been known, reliably attested, and treated with reverence by Christians for almost two millennia. To deny or question the "historicity" of their missionary work and martyrdoms is thus patently absurd.

The most important and comprehensive of these sources is undoubtedly the writings attributed to Saint Abdias of Babylon. Abdias (also known as Obadiah) was, according to venerable tradition, one of the seventy-two disciples sent by Our Lord to proclaim the Good News.[1] After the Resurrection of Christ, Abdias continued his work of evangelization, being ordained as the first bishop of the city of Babylon (located in modern-day Iran) by the apostles Simon and Jude. Because of this, Saint Abdias is recognized as the first Patriarch of the Persian Church.

Saint Abdias wrote lives of each of the twelve apostles (with the exception of Judas Iscariot), and also a life of

1 See Luke 1:1–24.

Saint Paul. While these lives do not have the authority or status of canonical Scripture, it is wrong to dismiss them for this reason as "merely apocryphal." While they are not part of the canon of Scripture, they nevertheless remain genuine and useful ancient documents. Their historical importance and interest to all Christians is very great indeed, since the apostles are rightly described by Scripture itself as the stones on which the Church itself is built.[2]

There are indeed compelling reasons to trust in the reliability of the apostolic histories written by, or attributed to, Saint Abdias. There is a great consistency between their contents and all the various other existing accounts and traditions. And the narratives attributed to Abdias accord closely with what is known of the early history of the Church in the different localities where the various apostles proclaimed the Gospel. These localities include not only Rome, but also Ethiopia, Armenia, Persia, and India, all of which have strong and detailed traditions of their own local Church's history, extending back to apostolic times.

In the case of the biographies of Saint Peter and Saint Paul, the various places and names given all match closely with long-standing Roman traditions. This internal consistency is powerful evidence of the veracity and reliability of these narratives. For example, the places of the execution and burial of both Saint Peter and Saint Paul

---

2 See Ephesians 2:20 and Revelation 21:14.

are long-standing parts of the history of Rome, and can be visited and seen to this present day.

The stories of the missionary work and martyrdom of Saint Peter and Saint Paul are both exciting and highly edifying. Readers will encounter Saint Peter's dramatic "showdown" with the wicked sorcerer Simon Magus, and will discover Saint Paul's eloquent and bold speech made before the deluded and megalomaniacal emperor, Nero. They will learn the unforgettable details of the martyrdom, by crucifixion and beheading respectively, of these two holy and brave men.

It is the sincere hope of the translator that these unique, compelling, and valuable writings may be a source of inspiration for modern Catholics, and may help to fill in the regrettable lacunae in knowledge which exists among many contemporary Catholics on the mission and martyrdom of Saint Peter and Saint Paul.

Sancte Petre et Sancte Paule, orate pro nobis!

Fr. Robert Nixon, OSB,
Abbey of the Most Holy Trinity,
New Norcia, Western Australia

The Life and Martyrdom of Saint Peter

HGB

Chapter 1

After the coming in the flesh of the eternal Word of God, Our Lord Jesus Christ, the true light of the world, which was Christ Himself, illuminated the darkness that engulfed the cosmos.

Once, while Christ was walking by the Sea of Galilee, He saw there two brothers, Simon (who was to be called Peter) and Andrew. They were casting their nets into the sea, for they were fishermen.

The Lord spoke to them, saying in a soft but commanding voice: "Follow me, and I shall make you to become fishers of men." And, sensing the mysterious authority which emanated from Him, the two brothers immediately abandoned their nets and followed Him.

They walked on for a while in silence, and Christ was joined by certain other disciples of His. And after they had traveled for some time and had arrived in the city of Caesarea Philippi, the Lord Jesus Christ addressed to the group the following question: "Who do men say that the Son of Man is?"

They replied to Him in various ways. "Some say John the Baptist, others say Elijah, others say Jeremiah or one of the prophets," they said. But Peter, with absolute firmness and the courage of his conviction, raised his voice among the others, and announced with gravity, certainty, and dignity: "You are the Christ, the true Son of the Living God!"

Jesus, responding to him, then said: "Blessed are you, Simon, son of Jonah, for it is not mere flesh and blood which has revealed this to you, but rather My Father who is in Heaven! Therefore I tell you truly: you are Peter, and upon this rock shall I build My Church, and the gates of hell shall not prevail against it. Unto you do I give the keys of the Kingdom of Heaven. And whatever you bind on earth shall be bound in Heaven, and whatever you loosen upon earth shall be considered loosened in Heaven."

At about the same time, when Christ was about to spend time in prayer, He departed for a certain mountain, as was his custom, taking with Him three of His leading disciples, Peter, John, and James. And when they were on the peak of the mountain, a cloud of radiant light, with the brightness of the sun, shone around Christ, enveloping His body in its glow. He Himself became intensely and gloriously radiant, and His disciples perceived Him to be accompanied, on either side, by Elijah and Moses.

"Lord," exclaimed Peter, "this is a good place to dwell in! If it pleases You, let us build three tents here, one for You, and the others for Elijah and Moses." But Jesus did not offer any response to this suggestion. Instead, He encouraged them to rise up and to put aside any fear they might feel. And after that, He continued to speak to the three disciples, warning them about the things which would come to pass, including His own arrest, suffering, and death.

A little later, just before the annual celebrations of the Passover commenced, Jesus sat at table with His chosen disciples. And He knew at that time that all things had been placed into His hands by his eternal Father, and that He had come from God and unto God He was destined soon to return. And, when the supper was complete, He arose from the table and removed His outer garments. Taking a cotton towel and affixing it as a belt around His waist, He poured water into a basin, and then began to wash the feet of His disciples, drying them gently with the cotton towel afterwards.

When Christ came to Simon Peter to wash his feet, Peter, feeling himself entirely unworthy of this, said to Him: "Lord, You will not wash *my* feet!" But Jesus responded, saying: "You do not now understand what I am doing, but you shall understand this afterwards." But Peter, still feeling that it was not right for His Lord to perform this humble task of service for him, protested once more: "You shall *never* wash my feet!" But to this, Christ responded: "Unless I wash you, you can have no part with Me."

Upon hearing this, Peter then exclaimed: "Then, Lord, not only wash my feet, but my head and hands as well!" But Jesus said: "For one who is clean, it is not necessary that he be washed further, for he is truly clean already."

We have now completed our summary of the deeds of Peter before the Resurrection, all of which may be found recorded in the pages of the holy Gospel.

CHAPTER 2

AFTER HIS RESURRECTION from the dead, the Lord spoke to Peter during one of His appearances to the disciples. "Do you love me?" He asked him. "Indeed I do, Lord. You know that I love you." Then Christ said to him: "Then feed my lambs." A little later, Christ asked Peter once again: "Simon, son of Jonah, do you love me?" To this, he responded: "Lord, You know that I love you." This time, Jesus said: "Then feed my sheep."

Finally, a third time, the Lord asked Peter: "Do you love me?" Peter was surprised and somewhat saddened to be asked this for the third time. He replied: "Lord, You know all things. You *know* that I love you!"

To this, Jesus replied: "Then you must feed my sheep." Continuing, the Lord said to him: "When you were young, you put on your own belt and went about wherever you wished. But the time will come, when you are old, when you will reach out your hands and another shall place a belt upon you. And you shall then be led unto a place where you would rather not go!" He said this, signifying the kind of death which Peter would die, to glorify God.

This happened on that occasion when the Savior appeared to some of His disciples by the Sea of Tiberius. At that time, they were fishing on a boat, and the Lord appeared standing on the shore. He asked them if they had caught anything. The disciples, who did not recognize Jesus at that point, replied that they had caught nothing at all. When He heard this, the Lord told them to cast their nets out once more, on the right side of the boat. This they did, and caught a huge haul of fish. So great was the catch in the net that Peter dived into the water to help pull the overflowing net out.

It was only after this miracle that the veil which had covered their eyes was removed, and the disciples recognized the person on the shore to be Christ. Arriving on the shore of the sea, they found Him cooking some fish there on hot coals, with some bread beside Him. And the fish they had caught numbered some 153. Christ then invited them to join Him in partaking of the freshly-cooked fish and bread, and they shared this simple meal with Him.

These are the memorable deeds of Peter which took place after the Resurrection of the Lord and before His glorious Ascension. They are likewise recorded in the pages of the holy Gospel.

Shortly after the Lord had ascended into the Heavens, Peter and John together went up into the temple at Jerusalem at three o'clock in the afternoon to offer their customary prayers. And a certain man who had been lame since he had come forth from his mother's womb was carried there. Every day, he would be placed at the gate of the temple, which is known as the Beautiful Gate, and there he would beg for alms from those entering the temple.

When Peter, who was accompanied by John, saw this lame beggar, he said to him: "Look at us!" Then the beggar turned to them, expecting to receive some gift of alms from them. But Peter said: "I possess neither silver or gold, but what I do have, I shall gladly give to you." Then he proceeded to say to the afflicted man: "In the name of Jesus Christ the Nazarene, arise and walk!" And he stretched forth his right hand, and raised the beggar up. And immediately the lame man's feet and legs were made strong and functional. He stood up and walked about, and even leapt and danced for joy.

Then, after this miracle had occurred, Peter and John entered the temple. They boldly proclaimed the glory of the Lord before all the people assembled there. It should be noted that the man who had been lame since his birth and then healed through the prayer of Peter was already more than forty years old when he was cured.

The number of people who came to believe in Christ continued to increase rapidly, and by now included a great multitude of both men and women. And these would place large numbers of the sick and crippled out in the city squares and along the roads, carrying them on stretchers, wherever they heard that the apostles were likely to be passing. They did this in the hope of obtaining the benefit of a healing miracle; and, indeed, many of the sick and afflicted were cured through the prayer and sanctity of Saint Peter and the other apostles.

CHAPTER 3

WHEN THE STORIES of the miracles and wonders worked by the apostles, and Saint Peter in particular, began to circulate, a great multitude from the surrounding region began to come to Jerusalem, bringing with them all of the sick and crippled. And Peter, through prayer offered in the name of Jesus Christ, was able to cure virtually all of them.

At this time, the rumor spread to Jerusalem and to the ears of the apostles that the people of Samaria had enthusiastically accepted the word of the Lord. So the apostles sent forth Saint Peter and Saint John, who would be able to encourage the newly converted Samaritans, to preach the Gospel to them, and to ensure that they were properly instructed in the Christian faith.

When Peter and John had arrived in Samaria, they prayed with the followers of Christ there, earnestly beseeching God that they should be granted the Holy Spirit. For the Holy Spirit had not yet come upon any of them, for they had only been baptized in the name of Jesus, rather than in the name of the Father, the Son, and the Holy Spirit.

But when the apostles placed their hands upon them and prayed, each of them did indeed receive the Holy Spirit.

A certain Samaritan, Simon, who was known as Simon the Sorcerer, witnessed this take place and had observed these people to become filled with the Holy Spirit at the hands of Peter and John. He himself had already been baptized and had likewise received the Holy Spirit from the apostles, together with the other Christians of Samaria. But, not content with this, he was eager to acquire also the power of the apostles, to impart the Holy Spirit to others through the laying of his hands upon them. So he offered to the apostles a large sum of money to obtain this from them, saying: "Grant to me this power, so that whoever I shall lay my hands upon will receive this Holy Spirit!"

But Saint Peter firmly rebuked him, saying: "May your wealth become your perdition, for you have considered the gifts of God to be the kind of things which can be purchased for mere money! For this reason, you may have no part in this work which you sought for yourself. For your heart is not yet right before the Lord. Therefore, Simon, do fitting penance and seek to overcome this wicked vice of personal ambition. Ask the Lord for forgiveness, and pray that He may deign to free you from this harmful and dangerous impulse. For I perceive that your heart is still far from pure, and I see that you yet remain in the gall of bitterness and in bonds of servitude to iniquity, ambition and corruption."

Upon hearing this, Simon the Sorcerer, feeling a pang of compunction, said to the apostles: "Please pray to the Lord for me, that I shall be spared from these woes!"[3]

The apostles then continued with their work of proclaiming and preaching the Gospel in Samaria. And having brought about the conversion to Christ of many of the people in that region, they then returned to the holy city of Jerusalem.

After Peter had made the rounds of a great many towns and villages preaching the Gospel and teaching the faith, he came to the city of Lydda.[4] There, he visited and encouraged the local community of Christians, encouraging them by his presence and company and instructing them by his words and wisdom. Among the Christians in Lydda, there was a certain man named Aeneas. He suffered from paralysis and had spent some eight years confined to his bed, rendered completely immobile by his malady.

---

3 It is interesting to note that Simon the Sorcerer (Simon Magus) appears to have been genuine, at least initially, in his belief in the message of the apostles. His sin was primarily one of permitting human ambition and desire for personal power to affect his approach to faith and view of the ministry. It seems that, at this point, his repentance was at least partially sincere. See Acts 8.

4 See Acts 9:3235.

Peter visited him and said to him: "Aeneas, arise! Our Lord Jesus Christ has healed you." And at once, the paralysis left him, and he rose to his feet. He then proceeded to arrange his bedding, free at last from confinement to it.

Now, it was not long before everyone who inhabited Lydda and the surrounding coastal region of Sharon saw Aeneas, the former paralytic, walking about freely. Astounded by this visible and undeniable miracle, the majority of the citizens were then converted to faith in the Lord Jesus Christ.

At about this same time, there was a certain female disciple of Christ named Tabatha (whose name in Greek was Dorcas).[5] She lived in the city of Joppa, which is not very far from Lydda. Her life was filled with good works and the generous giving of alms, which she did on a daily basis. But it happened that she was struck by a very severe and sudden illness, and so passed away. After the body had been washed, her corpse was laid in an upper room.

Since Joppa, where she had lived, was quite close to Lydda, the Christian community sent two men to seek out Peter there and to urge him to come and visit them. They hoped particularly that he might be able to offer some comfort and blessing during their time of grief at Tabitha's sad and untimely demise.

---

5 See Acts 9:36–42.

Peter agreed to this and accompanied them back to Joppa. When he had arrived there, they took him to the upper room, where the body of the unfortunate Dorcas lay. There was a multitude of mourners there also, all in deep sorrow at her tragic death. And they lovingly showed Peter some of the vestments which the deceased woman had made, for she was a dressmaker by profession.

Peter observed the depth and sincerity of their sadness and grief and was overcome with compassion for them. Dismissing most of the mourners, he raised his eyes and hands to Heaven and fell to his knees in earnest and silent prayer. Then, arising, he turned to the body of the deceased woman and said: “Tabitha, arise!”

And immediately, she opened her eyes. Seeing Saint Peter before her, she sat up on the bed where she had lain. And Peter stretched out his hand to her and raised her up, so that she stood upright and alive.

Then he called back the members of the community of the faithful who had been mourning her. He presented her to them, now filled with life and vitality once more. And this marvelous deed of faith and power came to be known through the entire city of Joppa, and a great multitude were filled with wonder and awe and so came to believe in the Lord Jesus Christ.

CHAPTER 4

AT ABOUT THIS same time, the king, Herod, began to persecute members of the Church, being filled with fear that they would undermine his own power. When he saw that this persecution greatly pleased the Jews, he decided to have Saint Peter himself arrested.[6] Now, at this time, it was the days of unleavened bread, accompanying the festivities of the Jewish Passover.

After Herod's officers had seized Peter, he was placed in prison, and a team of four soldiers was assigned to the duties of guarding him, so that two of them should be awake and keeping watch at his cell at all times, throughout both the day and the night. It was Herod's plan to make Peter's arrest known to the public after the Passover festivals, and to determine how he should be dealt with at that time. But the members of the Church, who were already aware of the arrest and detention of the Prince of the Apostles by Herod, prayed to the Lord unceasingly both for his well-being and his liberation from the plight in which he found himself.

---

6 See Acts 12.

On the night before Herod was due to bring Peter before the public, Peter was sleeping, held fast in chains and guarded by two soldiers. These soldiers both stood awake at the door of his prison cell. And then, suddenly, an angel of the Lord appeared before Peter, radiantly aglow with a brilliant light. And so bright was this light that it illuminated the whole of the dark prison building. The angel aroused Peter from his sleep by striking him on the side. It commanded him: "Arise with all haste!" And at that instant the chains which had constrained the apostle fell from his hands and his feet.

The angel then instructed him to put on his belt and his shoes, which he did. It said to him: "Put on your cloak, and follow me." And the angel proceeded directly out of the prison doors, which miraculously opened before it. Peter, amazed and awestruck, followed him closely. Indeed, Peter did not fully comprehend what was happening, and suspected that it was all a vision or a dream of his own sleeping mind.

Passing unperceived and unhindered by both the first and the second soldiers who stood guard at his cell, they came to the gate known as the Iron Gate. This led into the city, for the prison itself was outside of the city walls. So Peter, led by the angel of the Lord, entered the city of Jerusalem once again, as a free man.

The next morning, when he had fully recovered his senses and was able to consider all that had transpired, Peter understood that it was an angel of the Lord who had freed him from prison, and from the hands of the wicked King Herod and the malicious and envious hatred of the elders and temple authorities, and all those people who had refused to accept Christ.

CHAPTER 5

AFTER PETER'S MIRACULOUS escape from jail, Simon the Sorcerer, a Samaritan by birth who has already appeared in this narrative when he sought to purchase for money from the apostles the ability to impart the Holy Spirit to others, began to emerge as a prominent self-styled spiritual teacher and leader in Jerusalem. He presented himself as someone great and standing apart from and above the other disciples of Christ. And he promised that all those who followed his own teachings would never be destroyed or dissipated.[7]

Moreover, he enviously desired to undermine the ways taught by Peter and the other genuine apostles, and to subvert and discredit their teachings as much as possible. So he organized a day on which he was to meet with Peter to

7 There is some evidence as to the nature of the teachings of Simon Magus, found in the writings attributed to St. Clement I. According to this, he continued to acknowledge Christ as the Son of God, but assumed for himself a similar status. He also espoused the view that the Deity represented in the Old Testament was a different God from that preached by Christ (and himself). This dualistic view was taken up by many early heretical groups in the early Church.

dispute with him before a multitude of the public. At that time, Peter was at the port city of Caesarea Maritima.

When the appointed day for the public debate with Simon Magus had arrived, just as the dawn was breaking in the Eastern sky, the prefect of the city, a man called Zacchaeus, went to see Peter. He said to him: "Peter, the day has come for you to debate with Simon, the sorcerer of Samaria! Make yourself ready. A great crowd of people have already gathered together to hear the proceedings in the city square, and are waiting for you. This Simon is there too, ready to go, and he has brought along a group of his own disciples."

At this point, Peter asked all those who were present to join him in prayer. There were at the time a few non-believers there also, whom the apostle politely asked to leave for a moment. He then said to those who remained with him, who were all faithful companions and friends of his, the following words: "Let us pray, brethren, that the good Lord will help me, in His ineffable and boundless mercy. This I ask through His only-begotten Son, Our Lord Jesus Christ, who, for the sake of the salvation of mankind left the Heavens to dwell among us as a true human being."

And after he had said this and offered earnest silent prayer of supplication for a time, he strode forth bravely and with resolution to the public square, where his bitter opponent, Simon Magus, and a great multitude of interested citizens awaited him. After patiently waiting for silence for a time, it was Peter who stood up first to address the crowd. He spoke to the assembly thus:

"Peace be with you all, who sincerely wish to be found seated at the right hand of God's holy Truth! This Truth was made flesh in the person of Jesus Christ, and so whosoever shall diligently obey the words of Christ thereby becomes pleasing to God, the Lord of all. But in becoming pleasing to God, it is not God whom we benefit, but rather we advance our own salvation and happiness. It is through Christ, the Mediator between God and man, that we are able to obtain the highest of all gifts, which is perfect peace and blessedness; and this we shall surely obtain, if we earnestly walk in the paths of righteousness and faith which He taught to us. Hence it we are very well and wisely directed to seek first the Kingdom of God and its justice.

"The other apostles and myself are all dedicated to teaching this righteousness and justice which Christ taught to us. For we know that it is by both earnest efforts and endurance in the path of righteousness and justice that the Kingdom of God is reached. And in this Kingdom of God there is found that eternal happiness and fulfilment for which the human soul longs. But for those who offend against this justice preached by Christ, there will inevitably befall suffering, according to the nature and degree of their transgression. It therefore behooves every individual to seek to know the will of God, and to do their very best to follow it in their actions.

"How foolish are those who desire peace but to refuse to amend their ways, when it is plainly these same wicked or misguided ways that are depriving them of peace and happiness! Our time in this world is very brief and passes by quickly. And then it is our deeds and our character, not our eloquence or our mere words about what we believe, that will determine our eternal fate. Therefore we should seek above all to conduct ourselves in such a manner so that we can know that we are on the path which leads to eternal life and happiness.

"My advice to you all is therefore this: seek firstly the Kingdom of God, which is everlasting peace and bliss, and know that this Kingdom is sought and attained only by following the paths which Christ Himself taught to us. This, as I said, is my advice and my judgement. But if there is anyone here who believes that he has a wiser or more correct teaching than that which I humbly present to you today, then

> let him speak! But in speaking, let him also give a fair hearing to what I have said, just as I myself promise to listen carefully to what such a person may say. In this way, let our disputations and discussions today begin and end with peace."

After Peter had concluded his speech and offered this gracious invitation to anyone who objected to what he taught, Simon Magus immediately stood up. Filled with arrogance and self-assurance, he responded in the following words:

> "We have no need for your so-called peace! Indeed, if we did have peace and agreement with you, we would not have advanced toward the real truth of the matter at all. For thieves and criminals and adulterers all have peace among themselves—but they agree only in their errors and wickedness. If we were to come to an agreement with you merely for the sake of peace alone, then we would not be helping those who are listening today at all. On the contrary, if we were to depart from here having arrived at a false peace and friendship with you, Peter, and with those of your ilk, we would be mocking and misleading all those who hear us!
>
> "For this reason, we do not begin our own case by calling for peace, but rather we honestly call for a fair fight, a battle even! If you yourself intended to fight

> error, you would not be in the business of striving for friendship with your opponents. And I wish you all to know that when there are two fighters facing each other, or two sincere opponents with fundamentally differing points of view, the result is not friendship; but rather that one emerges as victor from the conflict and the other falls as the one conquered! And so it must be today."

When Peter heard this, he was perplexed and frustrated by the attitude that the Samaritan sorcerer exhibited. "Why do you fear peace?" he asked him. "Do you not know that peace is the perfection and highest result of the law of God? Wars and battles and conflicts—these all originate from sinful human ambitions and instincts. Where there is an absence of sin and error, and an absence of wicked drives and compulsions and evil feelings from human hearts, the sure result is peace; and not only peace, but truth also then will clearly shine forth, with no errors to obstruct it and no wickedness to darken it."

But Simon Magus remained unmoved by Peter's wise observations:

> "There is nothing of truth, and nothing of any consequence, in what you are saying! But now, I shall display to you all the power of my own virtue and my

own divinity, so that you may trust and worship the God with whom I myself am one.

"I myself am the first in virtue and power, and I am united with the Deity who is eternal and has existed without beginning. I entered into the womb of Rachel, my own earthly mother, and I was born of her as a human being, and it is for this reason that you are able to perceive me as a man in the flesh.

"The miracles I have performed are countless, and attested to by innumerable witnesses.

I am able to fly through the sky as a flame of fire ascends into the air.

I am able to make statues move about and speak as if alive.

I am able to raise the dead to life.

I am able to transform stones into bread.

I can cast myself down from a mountain peak and fly like a bird safely to the ground, for the hands of the angels support me.

"And not only have I performed all these deeds, but know that I am able to repeat them right here and now! By this means, I am ready to prove to you the truth of what I say and what I claim. For I am a Son of God, a dweller of eternity! And I am able to make all who believe in my words and my teachings similarly to become heirs of life eternal.

"Peter, your words and those of the other apostles are vain, and you yourself are not able to establish their truth clearly. You are just like that wonder-worker, that sorcerer, who has sent you—a Man who, in the end, was unable to free himself from death upon the cross.[8] But as for me, I am able to make myself invisible to those who would seize me, and I am able to reappear openly when I choose. If I wish to escape, I can enter physically into the mountains, like a stone entering into soft mud. And if I were to hurl myself from the top of the highest cliff, I would glide down to the earth without harm.

"And not only this—but if you chain me up, I shall free myself easily; and, what is more, leave those who dared to enchain me themselves bound up! If you put me in a prison, I shall make the doors thereof open freely before me.

"Show to me any inanimate statue, a figure fashioned from stone or metal or wood, and, behold, I can make it come to life, such that you will believe

---

[8] This suggests that Simon Magus had by this stage come to reject Christ, or at least to attribute to him less significance than himself. Other sources suggest that Simon continued to venerate Christ, but presented himself as His successor or equal.

it to be a living human being! And I can make trees spring up from the earth at the sound of my behest and bear fruit according to my choosing.

"I can enter into the midst of burning flame, and be perfectly unharmed and impervious to their searing heat. And, at my wish alone, I can transform the appearance of my face into whatever visage I choose, so that you would never recognize me. I can appear as a young boy or an old man just as I prefer.[9] Indeed, I can take upon the appearance not only of other human beings, but even of the beasts, such as a sheep or a goat, at my will.

"My friends, reflect a little upon my greatness.

I can fly through the air like a bird.
I can transmute common substances into purest gold.
I can cause those whom I choose to become kings, and to be obeyed.
I myself am venerated as a lord and master.
And I am publicly given honor as befits a being of divine nature.

---

[9] Other ancient sources relate that Simon Magus changed his appearance from that of a young boy to that of an old man before the emperor Nero. The explanation of this, and the other apparent miracles and powers of the sorcerer, perhaps lies in some form of hypnosis; as well as, of course, the involvement of demonic deceptions.

"Yes, was there not a statue raised in my honor in Rome in a public place, and is it not today venerated as one of the statues of the gods or demigods?[10] So what more need I say? Whatever I wish comes to pass; whatever I desire to do, I am able to do.

"When I was a mere child, my holy mother, Rachel, once sent me out into the field to harvest some grain. But, as I held my sickle in my hand, I spoke to it, saying to the sickle: 'You go out and harvest for me!' And it did just as I commanded. And that day, I collected ten times more grain than anyone else who was harvesting. And often I have commanded crops of grain to appear from the earth, and they have appeared for me instantly."

When Simon had concluded this lengthy and arrogant description of his own powers, Peter responded:

"Simon, I do not dispute that you have performed some astonishing works, for many here have witnessed them. But do not confuse what you are with what others are, and do not confuse what

---

[10] The existence of this statue of Simon Magus in a square in Rome is recorded also in the writings of Saint Justin Martyr, and mentioned by numerous Medieval writers. A statue, believed to be the same one, was discovered in Rome in 1547, bearing an inscription, "*Simoni sanc[t] o deo*" ("To Simon, a holy god…"). However, the correctness of this reading and interpretation of the inscription on the statue is disputed by some modern scholars.

> another—namely, Jesus Christ—is with what you are. For He was not merely a miracle worker and a teacher, but the true Incarnation of God. That you are a skillful worker of wonders I do not deny, for there are many here who can testify to what you have done. But the Lord Jesus Christ, while He did also perform miracles, was no mere conjurer or performer of marvels, or even simply a healer. For He was the true Son of the immortal and eternal God, and also the true Son of Man. Him we worship as the true God, and rightly do we do this. But as for you, you are a magician and performer and nothing more, and also a practitioner of those dark and demonic arts which are very rightly forbidden!"

Here, Peter issued a civil but determined challenge to Simon Magus. "Simon," he said, "so that I may prove what I say about you—that you are a mere magician, indeed, a trickster—let us all go to your house. And there we shall find your instruments and devices of trickery and sorcery, as well as your grimoires and forbidden books on the dark arts!"

At this point, Simon became perturbed and anxious, for he knew well that if the people inspected his house, they would indeed see there the devices and materials of the magical arts he possessed and his numerous treatises on sorcery. So he began to curse Peter and utter angry blasphemies. Meanwhile, the crowd also became agitated and restless. But Peter himself remained calm and untroubled, lest he seemed to react to the blasphemies of Simon Magus. Rather, he urged him more firmly that he accept the challenge of permitting him and representatives of the people to examine his residence for evidence of sorcery, witchcraft, and trickery.

In the face of Simon's stubborn refusal to the saint's very reasonable request, the multitude of people present became yet more indignant. The sorcerer of Samaria was then forcibly expelled by the crowd from their presence, with only a single loyal but misguided disciple of the nefarious and arrogant wizard following him away.

After this had transpired, Peter once more gestured for silence from the people. Speaking gravely and earnestly, the noble apostle addressed them as follows:

> "My brothers and sisters, we ought to put up patiently with those who are wicked, knowing that God is fully able to cut them off at any time, but He prefers to let them continue until the appointed day He has chosen when all people shall be judged by Him. Now if God, who rules Heaven and earth and all therein, is prepared to put up with them with such great patience, should *we* refuse to do so for our part? And all who turn to God and repent will be forgiven, and we cannot know who will do this. As for us, who have

each undergone such a conversion, let us turn to the Lord on bended knees and pray."

After he had said this, the multitude all knelt in humble prayer. Peter turned his eyes to Heaven and extended his hands in supplication. With tears in his eyes, he implored God to watch over all those present and to give aid to all who sought refuge in Him. Once his prayer was concluded, he requested that all the faithful should gather together tomorrow. Then he reverently offered the sacrifice of the Holy Mass, and afterwards dedicated himself to quiet contemplation, as was his custom.

CHAPTER 6

EARLY IN THE morning of the next day, one of the disciples of Simon Magus came to see Peter. This was the same man who had followed the wizard when he had been forcibly ejected by the crowd the day before. This former disciple of Simon now cried out to the saint, saying:

"I beg you, Peter, please accept me, a miserable wretch! I now see that I have been sorely deceived by Simon Magus. I had formerly listened to him as if he had been the Lord of the Heavens, since his miraculous works had astonished and convinced me.

"But when I heard your words yesterday, I began to realize that he is precisely what you say he is—a person who is indeed skilled in sorcery and tricks, but certainly nothing other than a mere mortal man. When I followed him away yesterday, I was still felt loyalty to him, for I had not had a chance to reflect fully on your words and comments. And when Simon saw me still following him, he said that I was truly blessed for remaining with him. And he led me to his home, and invited me in.

"Around the middle of that night, he spoke to me, saying: 'I shall make you better than all other human beings, if you persevere faithfully with me until the very end.' Tempted by this offer, I said that I would do so. He then requested of me a solemn vow or pledge. After I had repeated the words of the vow he demanded of me, he gave me a goblet to drink. This goblet contained a most foul and unspeakable disgusting fluid—I know not what it was!

"He then gave me a heavy sack of luggage and ordered that I carry it on my shoulders. A certain crude seaman or ship's captain then arrived. Simon advised me that he was about to make a voyage to Rome and asked me to accompany him as his disciple and assistant. He told me that in Rome, he would surely be recognized and honored as a deity. And he said that I should share with him riches, pleasure, and glory beyond all my imaginings; after which he would send me back home, supported by a whole group of loyal disciples who would serve me as my servants.

"It was at this point that the truth of Peter's description of him dawned upon me with full force and clarity. This Simon was clearly no spiritual teacher

> nor even a philosopher at all, but rather simply a showman and deceiver, intent upon nothing but his own personal profit and advancement. So, wishing to separate myself from him, I begged his pardon, but told him that I suffered from bad pains in my feet, and could not possibly accompany him as he requested. At this point he became furious, and accused me of laziness and weakness. 'When you hear of how much glory I receive in Rome,' said he, 'then you will regret this!' After this, he departed with the captain to commence his voyage to Rome. But I remained, and, as soon as dawn approached, I hastened to see you, O Peter. Please, grant that I may be assigned an appropriate penance and forgiven for my foolishness. I have been grievously deceived by this charlatan, and wish to be reconciled with the true Church!"

When he had finished saying this, Peter asked him to sit and wait for a while in the courtyard. The apostle then went forth outside to consider the matter as he walked. He noticed that a great multitude of people—larger than the crowd who had been present yesterday—were assembled in the square close to his house.

Immediately, Peter called forth the former disciple of Simon Magus who had come to him for reconciliation. Presenting him to the people, he said:

"This man whom you see came to me just a little while ago. He himself has recognized and can testify to what this man Simon Magus really is—an ambitious schemer, intent upon his own self-aggrandizement and advancement. He can tell you, from first-hand experience, that Simon uses both forbidden magical arts and trickery to achieve his astonishing deeds."

Upon hearing this, and seeing that the evidence was irrefutable, the crowd was deeply moved and utterly convinced of the truth of all that Peter had proclaimed to them about Jesus Christ.

Knowing that he had accomplished his goal of bringing the Gospel to all those in Caesarea Maritima who genuinely sought salvation, the brave saint then resolved to depart from thence to continue his work of evangelization in the other towns and cities in the land.

CHAPTER 7

AFTER LEAVING CAESAREA Maritima, Saint Peter went forth into the city of Tripoli,[11] and there he stayed at the residence of a certain disciple called Maro. He found a square within the city which was well suited for public discussion, and arranged to speak publicly there. Now, such was his reputation and the interest of the citizens in the message he had to share that, on the appointed day, the people could be seen gathering in huge numbers to hear him. Indeed, they came into the square in such a multitude that it resembled a river of humanity flowing and gathering into one place.

Peter began his discourse by greeting the people in the name of almighty God, as was his custom. There were among those who gathered there a number of persons who were afflicted by demonic possession. As soon as the apostle began, the demons cast their victims to the ground and began to shout out to Peter, requesting that he permit them to remain in the bodies of those they occupied for another

[11] This is Tripoli in northern Lebanon, not the city of the same name which is the capital in Libya.

day, before he cast them out.[12] But Peter refused this request, and instead commanded the demons to come out from the bodies of those they possessed immediately. And this they did, leaving their former victims in full command of their minds and senses.

Among the crowd, there were also a large number of persons afflicted with diseases and ailments of long standing. When they saw the apostle's success in expelling the demons, they also began to cry out to him, imploring him to restore them to health. Peter promised to pray to the Lord for them and assured them that God had the power and the will to heal them. But he asked them all that before he did any healings, they should all listen attentively to the message which he had come to proclaim to them. And so the whole crowd heard him with great eagerness and enthusiasm.

At the end of his preaching, he then turned to God in prayer for the healing of all those present who were sick or suffering. And immediately they were indeed all restored to health, without exception. He then instructed them to sit for a while, together with the former demoniacs whom he had liberated, to recover their energies. And all the crowd

---

[12] While it may seem unusual that the demons who are about to be exorcized make this request of Peter, it is consistent with the incident in the Gospel in which a group of demons (who identify themselves as 'Legion') ask Christ to send them into a herd of swine. See Matthew 8, Mark 5 and Luke 8.

who were present and had witnessed these marvels and heard Peter's eloquent words were moved to fervent faith in Our Lord Jesus Christ.

After his time in Tripoli, Peter next set out for Antioch. In that area, he visited a certain island known as Aradus.[13] On that island, there was a temple containing within it a great pillar made from glass. This pillar was of astonishing height and beauty, and was believed to possess miraculous powers. People would come to it and touch it, believing that it could impart healing or other spiritual and physical benefits to them.

Peter visited this temple and saw there a certain woman who was situated at the entrance of the temple. She was asking those entering and exiting the shrine for their support in the form of alms. However, Peter could see no visible injury, deformity, or disability of her person which would cause her to need to beg for alms. So he asked her: "Woman, why is it that you are here begging for alms? What is the affliction or need which causes you to resort to begging, rather than earning your sustenance by working with the two hands which the Lord has given you?"

---

[13] The name of this island varies in different manuscript sources. Some have *Ancharadus*.

The woman sighed deeply. "Alas!" she said, "although you can see nothing wrong with me, these hands do not work at all. How I wish that I could use them according to my free will, but they are completely paralyzed! They look like hands, it is true, but they cannot do the things that hands should be able to do. It is as if they have died already, and cannot feel anything at all."

The great saint was filled with compassion at the poor woman's plight. Taking her paralyzed hands in his own hands, he earnestly prayed that God would restore strength and mobility to her dysfunctional members. And, indeed, they were immediately healed and regained their full abilities and movement.

Now, it should be noted that this woman was none other than the mother of Clement, who would later become a disciple of Peter, and then serve in succession to him as bishop of Rome.[14]

As well as Clement, two other sons of this woman, named Faustinus and Faustus, were also converted to faith in Christ. These two brothers then changed their names to Aquila and Niceta, to signify their new life as Christians. Her husband, who was also called Faustinus, was also converted to the faith.

---

[14] This incident is recounted also in writings attributed to this same Clement (who became Pope Saint Clement I).

When it came about that Clement and all his family (including his mother, father, and brothers) were about to depart from the island of Aradus, his mother spoke to him thus: "My son, before I go there is a woman to whom I must say goodbye. For she was my companion and helper during my time of disability, from which Saint Peter has now cured me. And she herself is also poor and paralyzed, and can do nothing to support herself."

Meanwhile Peter, who was due to travel from the island on the same ship as the family, overheard the words of the mother. He was deeply touched and impressed by the compassion and care that she showed toward her friend. So immediately he commanded that the paralyzed woman be brought into his presence. This was done, and a crowd of interested and curious onlookers at once gathered around. Peter addressed them as follows: "O Lord, if I am indeed a herald of the truth—and so those who are present may be confirmed in faith in You, O Lord, the one God who made Heaven and earth—in the name of Jesus Christ, let this woman arise from where she lies!"

And the moment he concluded these words, the woman arose, restored to perfect freedom of movement. She threw herself at the feet of Peter and poured out thanks to the Lord and to the apostle whose prayer had brought about her healing. And she gave affectionate kisses to her beloved friend, the mother of Clement, Faustinus, and Faustus, who had formerly been her companion in affliction, but who now rejoiced with her in the gift of faith and healing.

CHAPTER 8

AFTER ALL THIS had taken place and Peter had left the island of Aradus to return to the city of Antioch, he was planning to find an inn or hostel there where he could rent a room in which to live during his sojourn in the place. But the father of a certain family who was a loyal adherent of the Christian faith came to know of this and protested to him against this plan. "It is ill-befitting for such a holy man as yourself, Peter," he said, "to stay in an inn, when I have several vacant rooms and beds within my own house which I can offer you. Please stay with us as our honored guest!"

But Peter was reluctant to accept, lest he become a burden upon any of the faithful. But then the man's wife also joined in. Prostrating herself at the apostle's feet, she said: "I beseech you, do us the honor of staying in our humble abode! It is no trouble at all for us." Yet still Peter did not accept.

Next, the daughter of the family, a young woman, rushed out of the house. She approached Peter. She, too, threw herself at his feet and urged him to stay. "It is only right,

Sir, that you should remain here as our guest. For I tell you, that this day, your very presence has freed me from an affliction which has caused me great suffering for a long time!"

Upon hearing this, the saint enquired about the nature of the affliction which had troubled her. One of the servants of the household told him that the daughter of the family had been vexed by a certain evil spirit for a long time, and the actions of this evil spirit had often necessitated keeping her restrained with chains and confined behind doors. "Since the age of seven, this demon has troubled her," said the servant. "And for twenty years, no one was able to cure her. But now, the demon has left her, as you can see. She stands before her in her right senses. And the chains which had been used to restrain her now lie unbound, so that she is liberated both from the demon and from the necessity of being forcibly restrained."

Both the young woman and her parents were filled with immense joy and gratitude. And Saint Peter graciously agreed to remain with them as their guest during his time in Antioch.

CHAPTER 9

THE NEXT JOURNEY of Saint Peter was to Rome, the great capital of the world. By this time, the saint had begun to sense that the end of his mortal life was not very far off (although he was still in good health and spirits). His travels to Rome had been accompanied by Clement, who, as has been noted earlier, was converted after the apostle had miraculously cured his mother of paralysis through prayer to the Lord Jesus.

In the presence of an assembly of the Christian faithful in that city, Peter took Clement by the hand. Addressing the whole congregation, he said:

> "My brethren and fellow servants of Christ, listen to what I have to say. It has been revealed to me by my Lord and Master, Jesus Christ, that my day of death is drawing nigh. And it is my will and decision to ordain this man, Clement, as bishop of the Church in Rome. I know that I can commit to him with full confidence and trust the episcopal seat of this city, for his teaching and preaching are both in accordance with the

truth which I have ceaselessly proclaimed myself. He has been my companion for a long time now, and fully understands all that I have preached and taught. Moreover, he has remained with me in many difficulties and tribulations. Beyond all others, I find him faithful and diligent, committed to sacred studies, sober, kind, just, and patient. And he has shown himself heroic and brave in enduring injustices from those who have proved to be traitors and treacherous.

"For this reason, I hereby commit to him the power given to me by the Lord of binding and loosing, such that whatever he decrees to be bound on earth shall be considered bound in Heaven, and whatever he holds to be loosed on earth shall be considered loosed in Heaven. And I am confident he will bind those things which should be bound, and loose those things which ought to be loosed."

As the Prince of Apostles concluded this speech, he placed his hands upon the head of Clement in a prayer of solemn ordination, and then led him to the episcopal throne which he himself had previously occupied. Over the next few days, Peter instructed Clement in some detail about how he should rule the Church in Rome entrusted to him, so that he would fulfill faithfully and fruitfully the injunction which Peter had received from the Lord Himself: "Feed my sheep."

CHAPTER 10

IT WAS SHORTLY after that that the apostle Saint Paul also arrived in Rome. Like Peter, Paul preached the Gospel of Christ zealously. Thus it was at this time, when the emperor Nero Caesar ruled, that these two saints, Peter and Paul, were both in Rome simultaneously, both proclaiming the Gospel. Both were active as preachers and teachers of the faith, and so there was an amazing increase in the number of believers in the city. These early Christians in Rome shone forth for their piety, devotion, works of charity, virtue, and wisdom, showing the power and workings of divine grace within them.

But as for Nero himself, he came to be deceived by Simon Magus, who, as we have narrated earlier, had traveled to Rome impelled by ambitions for fame and fortune. Simon Magus had completely captivated and enthralled Nero by means of apparent miracles, which were nothing more than illusions wrought by clever trickery or by the services of demons. As a result of this, the emperor regarded Simon not only as a wonder-worker but also as a philosopher and herald of spiritual truth, and chose him as his own personal guide and teacher. Simon Magus promised the gullible monarch that, as long as he followed his advice, he would obtain great victories in war, dominion over many nations and lands, and prosperity and success in everything he undertook. Stirred up by this nefarious charlatan and sorcerer, Nero then conceived a bitter and irrational enmity toward the two apostles of Christ.

Although Simon Magus had acquired for himself a wide influence and great popularity in Rome, Saint Peter did not hesitate to rebuke and refute him publicly. The apostle exposed his vanity, trickeries, and sophistries. The light of truth, which was then radiating throughout the whole world by the apostles' missionary work, came to dismantle the darkness of error and ignorance and lead humanity to salvation, shone forth brightly through both Peter and Paul. Peter's words and efforts particularly helped convert many people away from their misguided trust and faith in the arrogant sorcerer, Simon Magus.

But, unfortunately, for Simon himself, he chose to adhere stubbornly to the blindness of falsehood; for he had come to believe wholeheartedly in his own delusions and philosophical fallacies, and had been deceived himself by those means which he employed to deceive others. For although he had clearly witnessed the genuine miracles and superior wisdom and truth of Peter in other parts of the world, he believed that, now in Rome, the situation was different. Indeed, he was so deluded that he actually was convinced that he possessed the power to raise the dead to life.

At around this time, there was a certain noble youth who was a relative of Caesar. This youth died suddenly and unexpectedly, and naturally, his demise was the source of sadness and shock to those who knew him, for he was a fine and promising young man. So his relatives, and in particular Nero himself, began to wonder and enquire diligently if there was anyone in Rome who had the ability to resuscitate the deceased youth.

The reputation of Saint Peter as a healer and miracle worker was at that time very strong in Rome, and many of the citizens, even those who had not yet converted to Christianity, considered him the most likely person to be able to restore the dead man to life. But there were some others who favored Simon Magus. And so it was arranged that both of them should be summoned, and they would each attempt to restore the young man to life, using whatever means they chose.

So, both Peter and Simon Magus were brought into the presence of the corpse, where many relatives of the deceased were also assembled. Simon was openly asserting his own superiority over the apostle, and claiming that he would be able to raise the man without any difficulty. When Peter heard this, he said: "Very well! If you are so confident of being able to succeed in this serious matter, Simon, then please, do it without hesitation. As for myself, I make no claims of my own merits, powers, or wisdom; but I do know that Christ, who exercises His power in response to the prayers of the faithful, is able to raise this man from death, if He so chooses.

Then, speaking to the gathered people, he said:

> "Now, I will go further to show my trust in Christ alone. If this magician, Simon, is really able to restore this man to life, then you are free to believe that I, not he, am the imposter, and I will accept the penalty of death without complaint or hesitation. But if, on the other hand, he is not able to do this, and it is in response to my prayers to Christ that the youth is brought back to life, then I want Simon to promise sincerely that he will accept and publicly acknowledge the truth of the Gospel which I and the other apostles preach."

All of those present recognized that this was indeed a fair and wise challenge on the part of Peter and perfectly reasonable. Simon Magus, for his part, also accepted the proposal—indeed, in view of his erstwhile boastfulness, he could scarcely refuse it without losing face before the gathering and before the emperor.

So Peter stood by quietly, as Simon first approached the dead man. Standing by the bed upon which the body rested, he began first to chant various spells, sorcerous formulae, and diabolical invocations. This he did quite openly, in the hearing of all those present. And, to the amazement of all, the head of the deceased began to move about, nodding and trembling and shaking! Those who were opponents of the Christian faith naturally tended to hope that Simon Magus, rather than the holy apostle Peter, would prove successful, and so joy and excitement began to emerge among some of them.

But indignation and disgust began also to arise in Saint Peter, for Simon Magus had shown his audacity and foolhardiness by calling upon demonic agencies and evil spirits to achieve his effects. Moreover, he knew that the magician had not actually restored any life to the dead man at all, but merely used these nefarious spiritual forces to cause his corpse to move in a purely artificial manner, for the sake of astonishing those present.

At this point, Peter spoke up. He called for silence, and then said:

> "Very well! If the soul and consciousness of this man have genuinely been restored, then he could speak to us. If true life had really been imparted to him, then he would be able to arise and walk around. But all that happens is that his head moves about! This

is a mere trick, moving part of an inanimate corpse about, and is very far from true restoration of life!

"To prove this is the case, let Simon move away from the side of the bed where the deceased man lies. If the body then continues to move of its own accord, then perhaps the young man does possess life of his own. But if the movements of the head cease as soon as this charlatan and deceiver is removed from his proximity, you shall know for sure that it is nothing but a trick; for the mere movement of a dead body is not a genuine resuscitation to life at all."

Following Peter's suggestion, Simon Magus was then led away from the body of the deceased youth. And after this had happened, all movement of the corpse ceased entirely, just as Peter had predicted. Then the noble apostle, remaining standing where he was, closed his eyes and entered into a deep and intense state of prayer. Complete silence prevailed over the whole scene for some time, as the saint implored the power of God with all concentration and earnestness.

And then, in a strong and resonant voice, he said to the body which lay still on the bed: "Young man, I say to you, arise!" And immediately the youth arose, and began to speak. Needless to say, all of the man's relatives and friends who were present were astonished and overjoyed.

Peter then presented the young man to his mother, whose gratitude and wonder knew no bounds. She was very eager to repay the saint for the marvelous thing he had done for her, and asked him how she might reward him, for she was indeed very wealthy and influential. She assured him that she was willing to give him anything at all he might ask. "I ask nothing of you," replied Peter simply, "but that you act as a loving mother should toward your son, and take good care of him."

The crowd, which was present, having seen Peter's resounding triumph over Simon Magus, realized that what the apostle had said of Simon—namely, that he was a worker of tricks and had no miraculous powers except for those resulting from the invocation of demons—was perfectly true. Their anger arose against the sorcerer, and some of them wanted to stone him to death then and there. But Peter stopped them firmly. "It is enough," he said, "that Simon should acknowledge that he has been overcome, and that the message I proclaim is indeed the truth. Do him no harm, but let him live; and, whether he likes it or not, he shall witness the Holy Church, which is the Kingdom of Jesus Christ here, rise and grow steadily throughout the entire earth!"

CHAPTER 11

AFTER HAVING BEEN defeated by Saint Peter, Simon Magus had no choice but to acknowledge his loss. Begrudgingly, he admitted that it was Peter who taught the truth. But still in his heart, resentment and envy gnawed away and fermented bitterly.

So, shortly afterwards, the wizard of Samaria arranged to see the emperor Nero privately. He made a range of false accusations against Peter and the other apostles of Christ, disparaging them as ill-educated, uncultured fanatics and extremists, who wished to undermine the emperor's power.

Nero listened attentively to Simon. Even though he was fully aware of Peter's success in restoring his young relative to life and Simon's failure in the same undertaking, he still had some uncertainty within his mind and heart (for Simon was indeed highly convincing and persuasive). So the emperor decided to summon both men into his presence together, so that he could listen to each of them and evaluate their claims and merits for himself. When they both stood before him, Simon said:

"Caesar, I am surprised that you consider this Peter to be a man of any consequence at all. He is no philosopher or scholar, but merely an unlettered fisherman. His words and speech reveal this clearly, and as for his powers, they are overrated. Indeed, since he has shown himself to be an enemy to me, I shall summon my own angels to vindicate my dignity against this ruffian!"

When Peter heard this, he replied:

"Simon, I fear nothing of you and your so-called angels! For even if you do summon certain spirits, I shall compel them to fear me, by means of the strength and virtue of the Christ, the Messiah and Son of God—whom you claim to be yourself!

"Now, to prove that your boasts of being an incarnation of the Divinity are entirely false, I shall put you to the test. If God really was within you, you would be able to read the secrets of the human heart easily, for nothing would be concealed from you, since the Deity is omniscient, as everyone agrees."

Then, addressing himself to Nero, Peter continued:

"Honorable Sir, allow me to whisper what I propose to do directly into your ears, so that you, but not

Simon, may know precisely what it is that I am planning on doing."

The emperor agreed to this, and Peter went to him, while Simon was commanded to leave the room for a while. The apostle then asked the emperor to order a loaf of barley bread to be brought in and given to him. This was to be done in a concealed way, so that Simon Magus would not see what was taking place. Nero agreed to this small request, and so it was done.

Simon was then summoned back in, and Peter immediately asked him: "Simon, tell me what I have just thought about, and what has just taken place in this room while you were outside?"

This question greatly perplexed Simon, as he had no idea at all and could not possibly guess. So he said in reply, as if attempting to reverse the situation: "No. Peter, *you* tell me instead what I have been thinking about, and what I have just done!"

But Peter remained calm and said: "Certainly, I will do so gladly. But only after you, Simon, have first said what I have just been thinking and what I have just done."

Simon realized at this point that he would not be able to evade Peter's challenge, and so he turned desperately to Nero and said: "You must know, O noble Caesar, that no one is able to read the minds of other people but God alone! And if Peter claims otherwise, he is surely lying."

But Peter was quick to respond to this. "Simon," he said, "you assert that you yourself are the Son of God, and in perfect union of mind and spirit with the Divinity. If this is indeed the case, then you should also be able to read the thoughts of other human beings, just as He can. So tell me, if you are able, what I have said to the emperor and what has been done while you were out of the room!" Meanwhile, the apostle had carefully concealed the small loaf of barley bread beneath his cloak, out of the sight of the sorcerer.

At this point, Simon sensed that he was on the verge of being exposed and embarrassed before the emperor. Resorting to his skills in the black arts of magic, he uttered a malicious spell. "May the great hounds of hell heed my summons, and let them devour this man in the sight of Caesar!" And then a pack of huge black dogs appeared from nowhere and turned on Peter with slavering ferocity.

But the saint was completely unperturbed and raised his hands in prayer. And as he raised his hands, the dogs (whether or not they were real demonic hounds or merely an illusion) looked upon them, and then they utterly vanished.

Once again, Saint Peter addressed Nero:

> "O Caesar, you see what kind of man this Simon Magus really is—a sorcerer and a worker of empty marvels, rather than a true spiritual teacher. He asserted a

little while ago that he could summon angels against me, but instead he conjures up only apparitions of vicious dogs. And these vanish as soon as the true God is called upon!"

By now, Simon Magus was fuming with rage and frustration. He launched into a great tirade of his most wicked and diabolical spells, and then departed, shame-faced and angry, from the presence of the apostle and the emperor.

CHAPTER 12

But Simon Magus, far from being permanently deterred and converted by his exposure before Nero, became even more desperate and deluded. His pride, fed by anger and humiliation, now assumed the nature of insanity. In this insanity, he continued to deal with evil spirits and demonic forces, and, at the same time, almost came to believe himself to be a god.

He had it announced to all the population of Rome that he was going to show them that he was able to ascend to the Heavenly Kingdom whenever he wished to do so, and could, by the force of his own volition, go to the celestial realms as and when he chose. A day was appointed on which he asked the crowds to gather. Then he stood upon the peak of the Capitoline Hill, one of the Seven Hills of Rome. Climbing up to the top of a rocky promontory on that hill, he hurled himself into empty space, in the sight of all!

But, to the amazement of the crowds, he did not plunge to the stony ground below him. Rather, he actually began to fly through the air. The people were then filled with awe and fear. And many of them asserted that this was not a human power, but the action of a god; and Christ Himself, they said, never did such a thing.

Now, Saint Peter was among the crowd of those assembled. He was appalled by what he saw and saddened as he witnessed some of the people beginning to believe that Simon Magus was greater than Jesus. So he prayed thus: "O my Lord Jesus, show Your own infinite strength now, and do not permit these people to be deceived by the vain arts of this sorcerer, for the citizens of Rome are indeed destined to be faithful to You. Let whatever power permits Simon Magus to perform this trick (for it is certainly not by his own that he can do this) cease at this moment to help him!"

Then the apostle, knowing that it was demons or evil spirits which held the body of Simon Magus aloft, addressed these nefarious beings as follows: "You demons, I adjure you now in the Holy Name of Jesus Christ! Cease to assist this scoundrel in his trickery; depart from hence, in the name of the one true and living God!"

And as soon as Peter had concluded his words, the demons did indeed depart. The invisible wings that had carried Simon Magus through the air stopped functioning and no longer supported him in his flight. And his body plummeted to the ground, striking the earth below with a heavy thud. . . .

Needless to say, his body was severely damaged by this fall. His limbs were twisted and crushed, his bones were shattered in many places, and his skin torn apart by its collision with the rocky grounds. But Simon's death was not immediate—rather, he lay writhing in painful convulsions for a space of time, and then breathed his last and died.

CHAPTER 13

WHEN THE NEWS of the death of Simon Magus was conveyed to the emperor Nero, he felt sorely the loss of someone whom he had once regarded as a friend, a spiritual teacher, and advisor. This loss was of a two-fold nature—firstly, because of the demise of Simon, and secondly because of the realization that he had been an imposter and deceiver all along. The confusion, disappointment, and sorrow which fermented in Nero's heart expressed itself as a murderous rage against Saint Peter, unjustified though it was. And the emperor now began to seek a reason to have the Prince of the Apostles killed.

An order was therefore issued that Peter was to be found and arrested. Now, some of the faithful encouraged Peter to leave Rome in order to avoid being taken into custody. But was not swayed by their urgings, and refused to leave the city. He said to them: "I am here as an apostle of Christ, and I know that the Kingdom of Heaven awaits me after I die. Never shall I do anything to escape the death which is merely the end of this earthly life. For indeed, mortal death cannot be escaped at all by anyone, regardless of where one might go or flee to!" For Peter knew that all that befell him in the course of his ministry, even persecution, torture, and death, would eventually bring him to the eternal glory of Christ.

Peter's loyal supporters, who had encouraged him to flee, could not contain their tears and wept bitterly when they heard him speak thus. Now, the apostle was moved to pity when he saw this, for he realized that their anguish and grief were indeed profound. It was out of compassion for them, and not for any concerns for his own personal safety, that he agreed to depart from Rome. So that evening, after the customary prayers had been said, he bid his farewells to his brothers and sisters in the faith and went forth alone to leave Rome.

But when he arrived at the gates of the city, he saw standing before him Christ Himself. At once, the saint fell to his knees in loving adoration. He said: "My Lord, where are You going?[15] What are You doing here?"

And Jesus said to him: "I am going to Rome, to be crucified once more." When He said this, Peter realized that He spoke not of His own physical death, but rather He

---

[15] There is to this day in Rome, along the old Via Appia, a place which displays the inscription "*Domine, quo vadis*?" ("Lord, where are you going?"), which is believed to be the location of where Peter experienced this remarkable vision. There is also a stone which bears a footprint, believed to be that of Christ, on which He stood when this occurred. This stone is now housed at the Basilica of St. Sebastian (known as the 'Basilica of St. Sebastian Outside the Walls'), on the Via Appia Antica.

was saying that He was destined to suffer with and through Himself, His apostle and friend, in a death like His own. And so Peter grasped that it was surely his destiny to be arrested by the authorities and put to death by crucifixion, just as had happened already to his Lord and Master. Turning back, he then bravely returned to the city of Rome, knowing full well that martyrdom awaited him there.

It was not long before Peter was arrested and brought before Nero. The emperor, blaming him for the death of Simon Magus, then sentenced him to death by crucifixion.

When the news of this sentence spread through the population, a huge multitude of people, of all ages and both men and women, gathered in the city square. So vast was the crowd that the square could not contain them all. And, as if with one heart and voice, they protested against this clear injustice against a man whom the citizens in general, both Christians and non-Christians, regarded as good, noble, and holy. "Why is Peter to be killed?" they demanded. "What crime has he committed, or in what way has he harmed our great city? It is very wrong to condemn the guiltless. And we should be cautious, lest in harming this pious and sincere man we incur the wrath of the God of the Christ in whom he trusts."

But Peter himself spoke to the people and attempted to calm their agitation and mitigate their increasing fury against Nero. He said:

"Men of Rome, and especially you who believe in Christ and place your hopes in Him, be mindful of the gentleness and patience which He Himself practiced and preached. Take consolation in the various signs and healings which God has deigned to work through me, His unworthy servant. You must not doubt that Christ will come again; only, you must wait with patience. He will then repay all persons according to their works, giving each one what they deserve. And it is God alone, not you, who knows what each one deserves!

"As for me, I once witnessed my own Lord and Master, Jesus Christ, being betrayed and unjustly put to death; and He always taught that the disciple was not above his Master, and that whatever the Master underwent, His disciples could expect to undergo the same kind of things. And you should know that it is to my same beloved Lord that I know will soon depart. Why indeed should I delay my departure, and not rather hasten to the cross, for it shall be my entrance into glory and eternal life? Yes, even though my enemies may have captured my body and may destroy that, my immortal soul clings to God and cannot be separated from the splendors and bliss of His boundless love!"

Peter was then led to the place of execution by the guards. He asked them that he should be affixed to the cross upside down, with his feet upwards and his head downwards. For he said, it was not fitting that he, a humble servant, should be killed in the same manner as his Lord. And so it was done.

While the apostle hung upon this cross (turned upside down, as he had requested), he raised his voice and spoke aloud:

> "O, profound mystery of the cross—mystery beyond all words! This is the chain of love, the bond which can never be broken. It is the Tree of Life, on which the Lord Jesus Christ was raised up to draw all people, and all the universe, to Himself! On the cross was death itself put to death, and every human soul and the entire world freed from the bonds of everlasting death. It is a gift beyond all compare, and a revelation of a love which embraces all things and all people!
>
> "I give thanks to You, Lord Jesus Christ, Son of the living God; I give You thanks not only with my voice and my heart, but with my spirit too. It is in and through You that I love; it is in and through You that I speak; it is in and through You that I think; and it is in and through You that I see the world.

"You are all to me, and in all that I have and see and experience I know there is really nothing but You. For me, nothing exists but You alone, and all that exists is nothing but a revelation of You. You are the true Son of the true God. To You, O Christ, with the eternal Father and Holy Spirit, be all glory and honor forever and ever!"

And as Peter concluded this earnest prayer, all the people responded with a solemn and heartfelt "Amen," speaking as if with one voice and one soul. And then the noble saint gave forth his spirit and died.

One of his disciples, a man named Marcellus, immediately took the body from the cross with his own hands, not waiting for official permission to be granted. With precious spices and perfumes, it was made ready for burial and then placed in a tomb which was his own, in a place known as the Vatican.[16] This place is near the Via Triumphalis.[17] And the body of Saint Peter remains there in peace, where it is venerated by all the people of Rome.

---

[16] The ancient Vatican Hill (one of the Seven Hills of Rome) is now the location of St. Peter's Basilica, where the remains of the saint are located today.

[17] The Via Triumphalis ('Triumphant Way') is now known as the Via Trionfale.

THE LIFE AND MARTYRDOM OF SAINT PAUL

CHAPTER 1

THERE WAS ONCE a man who lived in Jerusalem, who was of the tribe of Benjamin, and the name of this man was Saul. He was extremely learned in the books of Moses and all the ceremonies of the Jewish law and tradition. Yet he did these all merely in accordance with the letter and sensed nothing mystical within them.

It was because of his adherence to the strict letter of the Jewish law that this man, Saul, was led to wage a campaign of tremendous devastation upon the early Church in his city. He would enter into the houses of the faithful and cast both men and women into prison, in accordance with the dictates of the Temple authorities. And he breathed forth threats and murderous hostility against all the apostles of the Lord.

In due course, Saul approached the High Priest of the Temple at Jerusalem, seeking from him letters addressed to the authorities of the synagogues located in Damascus. These letters, which he requested, would grant him power to arrest followers of the way of Christ there, both men and women, and bring them to Jerusalem to be detained in the Temple dungeons. And the High Priest, persuaded by Saul's zeal and determination, granted him the requested letter of authorization.

And so it was that Saul made the long journey to Damascus.[18] But as he traversed the desert plains and came toward the city of his destination, suddenly a radiant cloud of light from Heaven encompassed him. He fell to the earth and heard a voice saying to him: "Saul, Saul, why do you persecute Me? It is hard for you thus to kick against the goad!"

Upon hearing this mysterious and powerful voice, Saul responded in bewilderment and awe: "Who are you, Lord?" And the voice answered: "I am Jesus, the One whom you persecute! But arise and enter the city. There you shall be told what you must do."

The men who were with him were all astonished to hear this voice, yet none of them perceived the shining light. Saul arose at once from the earth and opened his eyes (for he had closed them to shield in the presence of the overwhelming brightness). And he then found himself to be utterly bereft of his vision, having been rendered blind by the intensity of the light. It was thus necessary for his companions to guide him by hand, and they led him to his destination of Damascus, which at that stage was already nearby.

---

[18] See Acts 9.

Saul remained in that city for the next three days, continuing to be afflicted by blindness. During this time, he devoted himself to intense prayer and reflection, neither eating nor drinking at all.

Now, in Damascus, there was a certain follower of the way of Christ, a good and faithful man called Ananias.[19] At about this time, the Lord appeared to him in a vision, and said simply: "Ananias!"

Ananias, instantly alert and ready to hear and obey, replied: "Lord, here I am!"

And the Lord then said to him: "Arise, and go forth to the street which is called 'Straight Street.' In the house of a man called Jude, which is located on that street, look for a certain Saul of Tarsus. For this man, Saul, is there at the moment, praying and awaiting Me. He is at present blind. But you are to lay your hands upon him, and then his vision shall be restored."

At this point, Ananias responded: "Lord, I have heard a lot about this man, Saul, already, and how much harm he has done to Your saints in Jerusalem. And he now has authorization from the high priests to arrest anyone who calls upon Your name here."

---

[19] This Ananias is believed to have been one of the 72 disciples (like St. Abdias, the author of this work.) He became the first bishop of Damascus and eventually suffered death by martyrdom. His feast day is celebrated on the same date as that of the Conversion of St. Paul (January 25).

The Lord answered: "Go forth, for this Saul, although it is true that he has been a zealous persecutor of My disciples, shall become for Me a chosen vessel. Yes, he shall proclaim My name to the nations, and to kings, and to the sons of Israel. And I, for my part, will reveal to him just how much he will undergo and suffer for the sake of My name."

And so Ananias, obedient to the voice of God, went forth to the house of Jude on Straight Street, as directed. Placing his hands upon Saul, who still lay blinded, he said: "Brother Saul, the Lord Jesus, whom you saw on your journey here, has sent me to you, so that you may receive again your vision and be filled with His Holy Spirit!"

And immediately something akin to scales fell from Saul's eyes, and he was able to perceive the light once more. Arising from where he lay, he was baptized into the faith by Ananias. And then he took some food, and little by little his strength was restored.

Chapter 2

Saul, with his sight restored, then remained in Damascus for some days, staying with the various disciples of Christ who resided there. Throughout all of the synagogues, he boldly preached the name of Jesus and testified that He was the true Son of the living God. When people heard Saul preach in this way, they were utterly astonished. They all said to each other: "Is this not the same man who fought against the followers of this new faith so furiously in Jerusalem, and persecuted all who invoked this name which he himself is now preaching? And, surely, he came to our own city for no other purpose than arresting the followers of this way and bringing them before high priests!"

But Saul continued to confound the Jews of Damascus by affirming unceasingly that Christ really was the Son of God. And, after some time had elapsed, those Jews who were most opposed to the Gospel met together and discussed how they could remove the influence of Saul from their presence. And they decided to have him killed. This plan soon became known to Saul himself. The Jews organized for men to keep watch at all the gates of the city, so that this new preacher of Christ could not escape from their power.[20] But some of the disciples came to Saul's assistance, and one night, they secretly lowered him from the walls of the city, under the cover of dark, concealing him within a large basket.

Afterwards, when he had returned to Jerusalem, Saul attempted to attach himself to the community of Christ's followers there. But they feared him and were reluctant to accept him; for some of them did not believe that he had truly been converted, but rather suspected that he was still intent upon their destruction, and wished to infiltrate their community to bring about its demise. But a certain disciple, a man by the name of Barnabas, related to them how Christ had appeared and spoken to Saul as he traveled to Damascus. He was able to attest to the genuineness of Paul's conversion and how he had preached Christ fervently in Damascus, and even at the risk of his own life.[21] The

---

[20] It should be noted that, although the city of Damascus was part of the Roman Empire, the Romans would delegate some authority to a local ruler of given ethnic groups (known as an 'ethnarch') who would then have certain powers over members of their own race or culture. It is in this context that Saul himself was given authority to arrest, from among the Jewish people, the followers of Christ. However, the plot by certain Jews to assassinate Paul would certainly not have been permissible under Roman rule.

[21] According to certain traditions, Barnabas already knew Paul personally and so could offer this evidence with assurance. Both had been

evidence and support of Barnabas prevailed, and thus Saul was accepted into the ranks of the Christian community.

---

students of Gamaliel, a rabbi who had taught moral principles of forgiveness and charity, closely resembling those espoused by Christ Himself.

CHAPTER 3

AFTER HE HAD been accepted by the Church in Jerusalem, Saul, who was also known as Paul, came to prefer to use this latter name. He continued to evangelize unceasingly, travelling through a great many cities to do this.

In due course, he came to Lystra.[22] In that city, there was a certain cripple who had been without the use of his feet since his birth and had never once walked in his life. When this crippled man heard Paul speaking, he gazed at him intently, attentive to the words he spoke concerning the power of Christ to save and to heal. Paul perceived that the crippled man had strong faith in his heart, and so he said to him: "Arise, and stand up on your feet!" And immediately the man arose. Leaping up, he began at once to walk about. The crowd, who knew the formerly lame man well, were all astonished. Crying out in a loud voice, they proclaimed: "This man, Paul, is certainly a minister of the same God who has performed many similar wonders recently in

[22] A city in Asia Minor, in what is now Turkey.

Jerusalem!" They were referring, of course, to the works of Jesus Christ, which were well and widely known by then.

And they told Paul also about a certain female slave or servant girl, who was able to foretell the future, guided by a certain demon. Her ability to do this had been ruthlessly exploited by her masters, who had accrued considerable profits thanks to her prognostications. This young woman, they told Paul, had been following him about, and crying out aloud: "These men" (meaning Paul and his companions) "are servants of the most high God, and what they are teaching to you is indeed the way of salvation."

Although she spoke truly in saying this, Paul was nevertheless deeply concerned at her words.[23] He said to the spirit which imparted to the girl the power of prophecy: "In the name of Christ, I order you to depart from this person." And immediately the evil spirit left her.

Shortly after this, Paul [traveled to Ephesus].[24] He remained there for two years. During this time, he, along with a number of other disciples from Asia Minor, would regularly dispute with their opponents and expound their faith and doctrines in the academy of a certain learned

---

[23] Johanne Fabricius, the editor of the Latin text of this work, suggests that the reason Paul was upset was that the devil was presuming to act as an evangelist himself here. However, it seems more likely to the present translator that Paul's concern was for the spiritual well-being of the girl herself, through whom the demon was acting. See Acts 16.

[24] This detail has been added to the translation, on the basis of the events related in Acts 19. Its omission from the original text is perhaps a simple oversight.

scholar called Tyrannus. And because of this, all who were in Asia Minor, both the Jews and the pagans, came to hear the word of God.

During his time in Ephesus, a great many miracles were performed by God through the hands of his chosen vessel, Paul. The sick and suffering were taken to him in great numbers, and by virtue of his prayers and the imposition of his hands, their afflictions and ailments were cured, and whatever evil spirits were vexing them were put to flight. And so his reputation grew, and many were converted through his efforts.

It happened, while at Ephesus, that one Sabbath evening we all came together for the breaking of bread.[25] Paul, who was there, was engaged in dispute and discussion with a number of pagans who were interested in philosophy and the life of the soul. This conversation was fruitful and prolonged. Paul, and all of us there, were quite happy for the discussion to be extended until the next day, and so it continued into the middle of the night.

25 It is interesting to note that the author, Saint Abdias, speaks in the first person here. Clearly, he was personally present among this gathering of Christians at Ephesus. This is by no means surprising, for he, like St. Luke, the author of the Acts of the Apostles, was one of the 72 disciples sent forth by Christ. And it is clear from the text of Acts that St. Luke was also present with the community on the occasion of this miracle. See Acts 20:7–12.

Now, there were many lamps lit in the upper room where we were gathered, to provide illumination in the darkness. A certain youth called Eutychus was there, seated on a windowsill. After the lengthy discussion that had taken place, a heavy slumber overtook Eutychus, and he fell asleep. Situated as he was, in succumbing to sleep, he also fell from the windowsill where he sat, tumbling down some three floors to the earth below. We hurried to attend to him, and, sadly, found him to be dead from the force of the impact.

Paul likewise rushed down to see the young man. Seeing his misfortune, the saint was filled with great compassion. Embracing the dead body of the youth, he prayed earnestly. Then he spoke to everyone gathered there: "Do not be disturbed," he said reassuringly, "for his soul has not yet departed from him, and is still within his body."

After this, we returned to the upper room and continued with the breaking of bread. After we had partaken of this, the conversation was resumed as before, continuing until sunrise. At this time, the youth who had fallen from the window was led back to the gathering, now fully alive and well. Needless to say, the rejoicing and relief among those present was not inconsiderable.

Chapter 4

After this miracle at Ephesus, Paul, determined to continue his missionary work to other peoples, went abroad on a ship and sailed to the island of Malta.[26] The natives of this island, though they were a primitive people, offered us their hospitality in a generous way.

Once it happened there that it became very rainy and cold, and so they built a large fire. Paul was assisting them by gathering wood. And as he placed this upon the burning fire, a viper suddenly leapt out and bit him, affixing itself firmly to his hand by its venomous fangs. When the natives of the island saw this, they were horrified. Some of them said among themselves: "This man must surely be a murderer who has sought to escape justice by the sea. Yet divine justice has not permitted him to live!"

But Paul, remaining perfectly calm, casually shook the serpent from his hand and cast it into the fire. Now, the natives looked on, fully expecting him to start welling up and very soon to fall over dead, for this was the usual result

[26] See Acts 28:1–10.

of a bite from such a reptile. But this did not happen—on the contrary, Paul was clearly completely unharmed by the venom of the viper. Amazed at this, some of them then began to say to each other in wonderment that me must surely be no mortal man, but a god.[27]

On that island, there was a certain wealthy leader of the people, Publius by name. We were received hospitably at his residence, and remained there for some three days. The elderly father of this Publius was gravely afflicted with fever and dysentery at that time. Paul consented to see him, and laying his hands upon him, he earnestly prayed for his healing. And the old man was at once cured of all traces of the fever. After news of this had circulated, all those on the island who were suffering from any kind of sickness or disease came to Paul, and he cured them all. And the people came to show every form of honor to the saint, and to esteem deeply both his miraculous works and sanctity. They gladly accepted the Good News he proclaimed, and the entire population of the island of Malta was converted to the Christian faith.

---

[27] A mistaken identification of Paul as a divine being is also described as having taken place at Lystra, in Acts 14. What is mentioned here is clearly a somewhat different case. In Acts 14, the people wish to offer sacrifice to Paul, believing him to be Hermes, and Barnabas, his companion, to be Zeus. In this instance, no mention of sacrifice or veneration is made—the comment seems rather to reflect astonishment and confusion on the part of people from a polytheistic background.

Paul next departed from Malta and sailed for Rome. There he remained for some two years, making his abode in a rented residence. And he happily received all who came to him, preaching the Kingdom of God and teaching all who would listen about the Lord Jesus Christ.

CHAPTER 5

IT WAS DURING this time that Paul resided in Rome and proclaimed the Gospel there that Saint Peter, who was also in that great city, came to be executed by crucifixion. This came about after Peter's confrontation with Simon Magus, which spurred the emperor Nero to fury against him.[28] But Paul, for his part, remained free at that time. For it was indeed part of the divine plan that Paul should not face martyrdom at that point, so that he could continue to preach the message of Jesus Christ to the people of Rome.[29]

And so it was that Paul quietly continued his work of evangelization with very fruitful results. But eventually this came to the attention of Nero. Various opponents and enemies of Paul told the emperor how he was engaged in promoting new superstitions and stirring up the citizens

---

28 These events are described in the life of Saint Peter, in this volume.

29 Note that there are two traditions regarding the timing of the martyrdom of Peter and Paul. According to one tradition, both were martyred on the very same day in Rome. The other tradition is that they were martyred on the same *date* (June 29), but not on the same year. This second tradition, which was favored by St. Augustine, is here supported by St. Abdias.

to rebellious and seditious sentiments against the rule of the Empire. Nero was naturally alarmed at this, and so had Paul summoned to his presence, where he questioned him thoroughly on his doctrines and beliefs.

In the presence of the emperor, Paul spoke freely and fearlessly. He said:

> "The teaching which I share is the same as that which my own Lord and Master, Jesus Christ, taught to me. But these teachings cannot be properly explained or understood by anyone, except by those who are pure of heart and blessed with the special gift of faith. But I can truly say that the message which I proclaim and the lessons I teach are those of simple peace and of charity, not rebellion. And I have been speaking this word of peace wherever I have gone, not only here, but in all the cities and towns from Jerusalem to Illyricum.
>
> "What I teach people is that they should treat each other honorably and decently.[30] I have instructed those who are rich and exalted not to extol themselves and not to become proud. I have advised them

[30] Paul's description of his moral teachings here, which is indeed perfectly consistent with that found in his epistles, is intended to show that he was teaching nothing unreasonable or contrary to civic duty. Indeed, most of the precepts described by him here accord harmoniously with what was considered as morally commendable in Roman culture.

not to place their hopes in worldly riches, which are ephemeral and untrustworthy. And I have exhorted all people to place their faith in God, the supreme Deity.

"Similarly, I have taught those who are neither wealthy nor very poor to be content with what they have in life, knowing that sufficient food, shelter, and clothing are all that a human being requires to live well. And as for those who are poor, I have encouraged them to be joyful and not to grumble at their lot.

"I have taught children to obey their parents and to listen to and take heed of wise advice from their elders. I have taught those with assets and possessions to pay their taxes to civic authorities with diligence and honesty. Similarly, I have instructed those in business to remit whatever tariffs and tolls are due from them to government officials. And I have taught wives to love their husbands, and servants and slaves to be obedient to their masters.

"I have exhorted husbands to be faithful and constant to their wives and to the bonds of marriage. For just as a husband will punish his wife for infidelity, so will God Himself punish husbands for their infidelities to the sacred commitment of marriage. And I

> have taught masters that they should be fair, reasonable and humane with their servants or slaves. And I have taught piety and reverence to all, calling them to worship with sincerity the one, omnipotent, supreme God—the Deity who is unseen and whose glories are beyond all comprehension.
>
> "These are my teachings, O Nero, and these I received from my Lord Jesus Christ and His glorious Father, who is God Himself. He has called me to preach this message, and has declared that He will be with me in everything that I do, as the spirit which gives life and imparts righteousness."

When Nero heard all of this, he was astonished, for it was not what he was expecting at all. He saw that he had no choice but to let Paul go free, since there was nothing in his teaching which was remotely seditious or incendiary, but, on the contrary, it was all perfectly reasonable and in full accordance with civic virtue.

But a little later, Nero began to feel the flames of wrath burn in his heart again, as if promoted by some diabolic force or irrational madness. And so, for reasons which were not altogether clear either to himself or to others, he sentenced Paul to death, ordering him to be beheaded at one of the customary places of execution. He dispatched two of his officers, men called Ferega and Parthenius, to arrest the saint and take him to the place of execution.

These officers came across Paul preaching the wonders and marvels of Christ to an assembled group of people in a public square. He was speaking and behaving with perfect liberty and sincerity, as if completely unfazed by his recent appearance before the emperor.

When Paul saw Ferega and Parthenius drawing near, he turned his eyes to them and addressed them, saying:

> "Come to me, my sons, so that you may come to believe in the true God, and thus your immortal souls shall be saved. For this God whom I preached sent His only-begotten Son into the world, and raised Him from death to everlasting life, placing Him in His eternal Kingdom in Heaven. And all who believe in Him come to be co-heirs of this same eternal life and wonderful celestial glory."

The men were slightly surprised to hear this. Although they were employees of the emperor, they personally bore no ill-will toward Paul, but, on the contrary, were quite moved and convinced by all that he said. So they said to Paul: "We have come here sent by Nero, to announce to you the sentence of death which he has passed against you, and to take you to your place of execution. Nevertheless, we ask that you pray for us to the God whom you proclaim."

They also sincerely asked him that they should be baptized, and so be initiated into the faith which has power to bring about the promised salvation of which Paul had just spoken so eloquently.

Paul heard them with tender compassion. "My sons," he said, "come to my tomb after I have been buried. There you will find two men, Titus and Luke, who will be at prayer. These men shall impart to you the sacrament of salvation which you have so piously requested."

At this point, Ferega and Parthenius, together with the soldiers who accompanied them, led Paul off to the appointed place of execution. There he stood for a long while, face the east and with his hands raised to the Heavens in prayer. After this, he wished peace to all those who were present, blessing them in the name of God.

Then he knelt down and blessed himself with the sign of the holy cross. Without fear, he extended his neck, offering it freely to the blow of the ax of the executioner, who stood ready at hand to perform his grim duty.

The execution struck his deadly blow, and the head of the saint was cleanly severed from his body. But it was not blood which gushed forth from the wound, but rather pure milk.[31] When those who were present witnessed this hap-

---

[31] This pouring forth of pure milk in place of blood is a phenomenon which is frequently in the accounts of the deaths of the early Christian martyrs.

pen, they all marveled and praised God, who had bestowed such glory upon His apostle.

A certain female follower of Christ, named Lucina, took the body of Paul at her own expense, in a tomb located by the Via Ostiense,[32] about two miles from the city of Rome.

The saint suffered martyrdom on June 29th, two years after Saint Peter had been killed, in the reign of Our Lord Jesus Christ; to whom be eternal glory and honor, together with the Father and the Holy Spirit, forever and ever. Amen.

32 This is a road which leads westward from Rome, to the port of Ostia. The place of Paul's burial is commemorated by the Basilica of Saint Paul Outside the Walls, located on this ancient road.